www.ingramcontent.com/pod-product-compliance
Lightning Source LLC
Chambersburg PA
CBHW071640040426
42452CB00009B/1706

People & Programs:
Social Profit Biz Basics

*Everything I Needed In Business I
Learned in the Bathroom*

Thyonne Gordon, Ph.D

First Printing: 2014

ISBN 978-1-889210-07-0 PAPERBACK
ISBN 978-1-889210-05-6 ELECTRONIC

A Writer Space Publishing
4859 W. Slauson Ave. #299
Los Angeles, CA 90056

www.awriterspace.com
www.beyondstory.com

Honoring The Doers

Carrying the torch that founder's ignite.

Kai Tramiel & Molly Dirr
Outreach & Program Directors, CoachArt LA
Juliana Wells, Director of Programs, YMC
Gloria Davis, Executive Director Girls Club of LA
Toni Laudermilk, Retired Executive Director
Charisse Bremond, CEO Brotherhood Crusade
Jonathan Zeichner, A Place Called Home

* * * * *

And Dedicated To
My Lovely Daughter
Matthia B. Sales
*Find your passion and ignites
the spirit of doing.*

Contents

Introduction

In the first Business Basics for the Social Profit Sector book, it was clear how a better bathroom set-up correlated to a better business infrastructure. When social profit organizations are correctly formed and maintained, they are equipped with the best tools for a lasting solid foundation – all from hints taken from bathroom basics.

In this second book, you'll learn the best way to utilize your most precious resources – People and Programs. Follow these easy to read bathroom to business tips and invigorate your organization's People and Programs.

As a graduate of three highly esteemed institutions, you'd think most of my learning would be from classrooms, but what I found as I began to work in corporate America and beyond, was many of the lessons I learned came straight from the bathroom. This lesson would become a

tool in how I managed business efforts in the future.

It started when a mentor giving me guidance in my role as a new Chief Operating Officer at a social profit organization, told me to, "Start in the bathrooms." I was very frustrated with this advice because I really didn't understand it. Yet, something (probably not knowing what else to do) compelled me to consider it and when I arrived to work on the first day, I began assessing the bathrooms.

Imagine the surprise of the staff that my priority started in the bathroom. And, imagine the shock of my realization that learning about this business would come from such a discreet and unsuspecting place. Well flush me away (pun intended)!

Using these simple lessons will help you manage teams more effectively and assure your programs are in order to run your business more efficiently. It will also

help you grow your business into the prosperous space you desire.

The book is divided into three parts using concepts and ideas straight from the bowels of the bathroom. Learn about your team and programs in this easy to read guide that quite frankly, can be finished behind a closed door on a familiar seat – in the bathroom!

501c3
The Business of Heart, Head & Soul

In this world where business is measured by a Wall Street status or how much companies make and take, I believe a shift must occur. This shift is based on the heart of a business. I know, many might note business, as an entity, does not have a heart. I believe business is a creative energy of people giving it heart.

With every client that's served, dollar that's earned and vendor that's affiliated, a steady beat occurs that gives the business a conscious how and why existence. And the beats are measured such that when there is a misstep, it causes a skip in that beat – and accordingly damage to that heart and ultimately to the business overall.

Starbuck's was one of fastest growing companies in the '90s shepherded by Howard Schultz. When he left and the company's beat began to shift, it was evident that the heart of the company was no longer the same. With his return, he revived a socially conscious heartbeat and the company began doing well again.

That heartbeat is in every company and becomes evident as culture. Starbuck's culture happened to be a distinct care in product and customer service. The care extended to employees and through their customers. In his book, *Onward: How Starbucks fought for Its Life Without Losing Its Soul,* Schultz shares the story of an employee who gives a kidney to a regular customer. Yes, that sounds above and beyond the call of duty for any employee, but it wasn't just because that employee was a good person (and yes, they were great)--it was also part of the culture Starbucks created. Care for each cup of coffee and care for each customer.

When we begin to focus on the value of giving, as well as what we receive in return, we can grasp what a company's heart beat feels like. The idea is not so far-fetched. The giving begins with offering quality products and services for reasonable and fair pricing. It extends to being in sync with the communities in which our businesses reside and valuing the needs of consumers.

There is enough to go around--if we are not so greedy as to hoard the extras.

In this equation of socially conscious businesses, the industry that society has labeled as "not for profit or nonprofit" have the opportunity to lead the way. These organizations understand the cause and affect of giving, and the inception of 501c3 is formulated from the heart. These organizations prioritize giving as a means of operating. Yet, as much as 501c3's understand giving, they miss how to properly receive. A key element is evident in the label that begins with lack, and that

lack projects a needy trajectory instead of a confident life changing and affirming one.

The 501c3 space is the only industry first described by what is "not" done verses what "is" done. In this inaccurate affront to an industry providing on-purpose services and products, the public tends to view such organizations as poor and needy (just as much in need as the constituents served).

With this impoverished mentality it is no wonder the difficulty 501c3's have in acquiring funds for mainly excellent services provided for society to work more holistically. In general 501c3's are viewed as beggars and in truth, every business "asks" for something.

In my work in this space, I encourage organizations providing on-purpose services to stand up for their work with a strong heartbeat, which starts with embracing titles that better inform the work. Changing the labels that others have

put on 501c3's is the beginning of building stronger infrastructure, and empowering entire communities.

In this book series nonprofits are re-labeled as Social Profit Organizations as my personal way of correcting the "skip" in the beat of the heart in the service community. This is the beginning of the shift I encourage.

Join me in uplifting the powerful work of Social Profit Organizations as positive and inspiring, by choosing our words carefully and specifically focused towards making a difference.

Enjoy the series and I look forward to hearing your feedback.

Chapter One
People and Positions Matter

Bathroom: What are the tools used in the bathroom & how are they used?

Business: Know the roles of each person in your organization and the departments they represent.

In business, just like in the bathroom, every tool or person serves a unique and specific role that, when used effectively, provides the perfect experience. Bathroom tools include:

Toilet paper: The ultimate necessity to wipe everything clean once the job is done. Without toilet paper, you can't clean up your dirty work.

What is used to clean up your organization? What tools are in place and how are they implemented? Is there a

specific person who handles the job and if so, do they have what they need to be effective?

Plunger: If there's a blockage in the pipes, the plunger is your 'go to' tool to get everything working smoothly again.

If there's a problem, do you have a way to fix it? What tools do you use to move things along smoothly again? Who is in place to assure that the tools are used properly?

Shower Curtain: The shower curtain not only keeps the bathroom floor dry, but also keeps water in the shower or tub.

As you build your programs, what do you use to see if they work? How are your people used in each program?

Towels: Like toilet paper for clean-up, drying off with a towel is a great finishing act for part of your bathroom routine.

What's the last stop or completion area in your business? Are there evaluative tools and processes indicating everything done is fully complete? What measurements do you use?

As you can see from the previous sample tools, each tool serves a purpose when used effectively and provides the perfect bathroom and business experience. In the social profit world this translates to know your team and know your departments functionalities.

We'll break this down to represent the tools you need for people and the departments that they serve under. There are some key questions you should examine:

Ask yourself whom you need in the organization? What departments and positions do you have? Just like in the bathroom, you need a well- organized set of tools (or a team) with each person being responsible for their specific tasks.

What is each person responsible for? What does each person do? Who lays out the program and who cleans up? Who solves problems or unplugs things? Who keeps everything "dry" and running smoothly?

What specifically does your team need to get the job done? What type of skills do your problem solvers or accountants need to ensure the business is running smoothly?

As you think about the answers to these questions, it's important to understand the type of people you're bringing into your organization and that they understand how to be a part of your organization. This is where your mission statement and the policies and procedures come into play.

When team members know what the organization stands for, they can determine if they truly want to be a part of that

mission. As they learn how you conduct your work, there can be further buy-in.

Take for example how most fast food chains work. A uniform is required on a daily basis. There is a schedule that must be adhered to. So, if a restaurant hires someone with a flair for fashion, and they are totally against wearing a uniform or working within a scheduled time frame, what do you think will happen? Yes, that person will ultimately not wear the uniform or they will slice, dice and dye the uniform such that it will be unrecognizable! They will also, more than likely, not show up for work in a timely fashion.

Assessing and fitting employees into the right place in your organization is really an important part of having an effective team.

What's in a name?

People & Programs: Social Profit Biz Basics

The names we're given at birth identify whom we are or whom our parents thought we would grow into. You may have been named after a hero from your family or a warrior from a book, or even a celebrity that someone liked. Our names are important because they identify us. The same is true for your team.

Each player, on the team should know his or her role, in name and in description. Having a clear title, and job description that is equivalent does this.

Titles say a lot about your organization and the people that hold them. In general, when a person is given a title, it is often perceived as a level or form of status. Titles equate people to certain levels in the company. However, this can be a mistake in trying to build teams. When people are not caught up in titles for the sake of status, it creates a strong and solidified team that works. When your team understands the title is equivalent to their level of responsibility verses for status, they can

appreciate the value of having appropriate titles.

In the social profit arena, organizations usually use titles such as Directors, Officers, Coordinators, Associates or Assistants. Officers usually fall under executive management, while Directors act as managers who direct the actions of specific departments. Coordinators are generally more task-oriented individuals working under supervision doing things hands on.

Finally, Assistants support the overall work and care for the core, everyday, functions that need to be carried out.

Following is a list of some of titles and the responsibilities that may be found or needed, in your social profit organization:

Founder - *Visionary launching organization.*
Executive Director – *Usually Founder leading organization and in charge of entire*

operation from program and fundraising to being the face of the organization.

Chief Executive Officer *– Used interchangeably with Executive Director.*

Chief Operations Officer *– In charge of infrastructure including facilities, IT, security and often Human Resources.*

Human Resources Director *– Responsible for Personnel including hiring, retaining and terminating employees.*

Chief Financial Officer *- Acts as the main financial person for organization and is in charge of the accounting department.*

Development Director *– Lead person for generating revenue for organization and chief fundraiser and campaign creator.*

Program Director *– In charge of organizing and directing programs.*

Financial Director *– Works under CFO or leads the finances if there is no CFO.*

Facilities Director *– In charge of assuring facility and maintenance are in order.*

Operations Director *– Runs facilities, IT, security, synonymous with Facilities Director.*

Program or Development Coordinators support the efforts of the team. They work under department head.

Bookkeeper, Receptionist, Intern, Security, Janitor, Administrative Assistant, Program Assistant, Maintenance – These positions are direct supports for entire organization.

Every position serves a specific purpose in an organization and care for employees at every level is essential.

When I first began cultivating the bathroom business basics idea, I realized my bathroom lesson was about more than keeping the bathrooms clean. It was about every person that I worked with being cared for too. And the most important lesson allowed me to truly understand whether that person was the janitor or the board chairperson, they should be cared for with the same detail and attention. Without proper care, guidance and training, you will not have an effective

team and in essence you will not have an effective social profit. With proper care you will have an army of supporters.

Department Planning

To be effective, your social profit team should be organized by departments yet work together to maintain efficiency. In many social profits, the departments are separated into three to four main areas that consist of Operations / Administration, Programs and Development. Each department is responsible for a specific area in the workplace.

The **Operations Department** is normally the core of the business in terms of setting up infrastructure. It is where policies and procedures for the company reside and many times the administrative functions also are run through Operations. The Operations team includes clerical support, receptionists, human

resources, maintenance, transportation, security and financial people such as bookkeepers.

This team opens the building in the morning and secures it at night. They greet new visitors, direct people as to where they can receive services and take care of the facility. Most importantly these are the people who keep the numbers in order and the team functioning properly.

Because Operations has to do with the entirety of the business, you can say the Operations is the actual room where a bathroom is housed. It's behind this bathroom door that you find the inner workings of a bathroom and the 'what' entry point to your organization's success.

Operations keeps these tools in mind:

*   Determine appropriate sized facility or offices for the work you do and the constituents served.

* Contracting reliable vendors for products or services (janitorial, printing, copying, legal, office supplies, equipment, Information Technology).

* Solid and current hardware and software for computers.

* Secure Accounting software.

* Recordkeeping for human resources, programs and development.

* Flow charts and organizational charts that are clear on reporting.

Whatever you decide for Operations, keep accurate records and document everything. It is the documentation of your work that will ultimately, help you evaluate your company and showcase it to the world.

The **Program Department** is responsible for creating, implementing and maintaining the work and/or programs, of the organization.

'Programs' is essentially why you are in the business that you're in. It houses the services of your mission and amplifies why you exist through the actions of the work.

Whether you service youth, seniors or animals, the programs team provides the services for your constituents. A Program Director manages the programs team and the work to be done by the team. This person works with a staff to provide the most effective services for your clients. Once the Programs are defined, the team can then come up with how they will implement the tasks to get the job done. As the work is done, a methodology starts to form. This methodology will eventually play out as your way of operating the programs.

People & Programs: Social Profit Biz Basics

Programs are to your organization like a toilet is to a bathroom – it's the heart of 'why' your business exists. The basic tools for Programs are listed below:

- Outline of programs and the services provided.
- Curricula or instructions on how the program operates.
- Evaluative or measurement tools.

As important as Programs are for the organization to exist, there is no program without funds. And, when you speak of bringing in funds to operate in the Social Profit world, your programs are important but there must be a team that helps showcase them.

Bringing in the funds to operate in the social profit world mean all eyes turn to the **Development department**. This department requires people who can help with fundraising, marketing, and relationship building. Event Planners,

Grant Specialists, Marketing Specialists, and Development Associates each play a specific part here ensuring that your company has the funds to stay open.

In small social profits there may only be 1 development team member handling the functions of development. Whether big or small, the department needs efficient and effective tools to stay afloat.

A Customer Relations Management system (CRM) is one of the most essential tools a development department should invest in. This is where you track people who have supported (or potentially will support) your cause. A good development team works on building relationships, collaborations and sustainable activities to fund the projects an organization has.

Want to know how the toilet flushes or how to fix something in your bathroom? That's what your Development department is about – the

"how" to your business and every detail about your donors.

An effective way to share your message is with a *Brochure or Information Kit.* This printed material is essential to have in explaining the work you do. A good brochure includes information on how and why the organization was founded; what you do; and how your work is done. Brochures that include the impact your organization makes on the community or the constituents served, are even more powerful.

Phone systems (with the right people on them) are key operations, but in the Development office they can make or break the organization. Choose a phone system that has at least 3 lines open at a time so that you can take multiple calls. There should also be a good messaging system to take and retrieve messages. Finally, the person answering the phone should be personable and equipped with the information to assist donors, volunteers, staff and constituents.

Today, *Websites* are almost a thing of the past with social media and digital formats looming. However, to brand your organization properly, a solid website with standard organizational information helps the world know who you are and what you stand for. Include information from your brochure to be consistent and keep the site updated regularly. Potential donors look current information in your media.

The Development department encompasses so many aspects for branding the organization, it could be a stand-alone book. Be ready to adapt to new ways to share your message while staying consistent.

Hiring the right People for the right Program

As you can see, having specific teams with the right people are essential to growing your business. When getting these departments and the staffs in order, finding the appropriate people to fit the

roles they've been hired to do is of extreme importance.

Someone who doesn't like to engage or talk with people, should not be your receptionist. At the same time, a person who is very engaged might be perfect for programs and providing services or they also may be great at asking for money in development.

Assessing who is right for what job can be challenging, but there are plenty of resources that make it a bit easier. In fact, many personality profile tests have been developed to assist in "right fitting" employees.

Myers Briggs testing is one of the oldest forms of personality profiling describing psychological types as positioned by C.G. Jung. This test takes seemingly random responses of varied behavior and places it in an orderly and consistent way to perceive individuals and their judgment.

The Strengths Finder, by Gallup helps people determine what they do best through a series of questions in an on-line or paper format.

Finally, one of my favorites is through the group Talent-Dynamics. They offer a Trust test that allows each person in a team to understand the quickest and easiest way to get into and stay in their personal Flow. The best part about Talent-Dynamics is they also provide clear strategies and actions for teams to take based on their profile, to achieve a desired result.

Your team is your way to success. Know them and where they belong department wise. Train them, acknowledge them and celebrate them. It will pay off.

Business Basic Tool 1: Know your departments and have well defined positions for your team members.

Chapter Two
Leading In Flow

Bathroom: Water is the essential element that keeps a bathroom in flow.

Business: The leader of the organization needs to be effective and fluent – like water for success.

With strong programs and people, it's time for someone to step up and take the lead. A strong social profit leader drives the mission through the entire organization. The leader must be totally into the entirety of the organization. From working with the board of directors to being in the community that the organization serves – leaders need to be able to move from one situation to the next fluently.

Great leaders do whatever it takes to move the organization forward in following their mission and growing into their vision.

They know how to use the tools they have and act as chief storyteller, marketing officer, brand guardian, financial keeper and spokesperson for the organization.

To be a great leader requires an authentic quality to lead the social profit even more so than just managing it. A strong leader is equipped with analytical and technical skills combined with vision and passion to move the organization through each of its phases. Emotional competence helps put it all into practice.

Just like the water flows through every part of the bathroom, the leader flows through the organization and keeps it as a working united entity.

Finally, the strength of your organization depends on the strength of the people, and the leader must find people who are as passionate about the cause as he/she is. Yes, your leader must have the Human Resource abilities too.

So how do you find great leaders and people to support them? Review the following steps of recruitment:

Define: Have a clear job description with strong and clear titles. The job description has purpose, responsibilities, required skills, knowledge, education and experience that the position requires. Referral sources help identify people and are extremely important. To really identify the right person, include the salary range with benefits in the description. (It may be useful to refer to surveys found through websites like:
 www.cnmsocal.org/salarysurvey for help.)

Recruit: Search for employees (including the leader) through Internet sources like LinkedIn, Idealist and Social Profit affiliate organizations (i.e. Opportunity Knocks, Center for Social profit Management and nonprofitjobscoop.org). Also inform other organizations, you are looking for someone. Referrals are great ways to find good people.

People & Programs: Social Profit Biz Basics

Manage: Once you find the right people, classify them correctly (exempt, nonexempt, independent contractors). Provide personnel policies and procedures along with an employee handbook. Give orientation of company and responsibilities. Schedule evaluations. Be clear about performance measurements.

Compensate: Reward staff that are a highly valued members of your organization with bonuses, incentives, and pay raises. If you recognize their valuable contributions, they will continue to work hard for you.

People are the life force of any organization. As the lead "toilet" in charge of the flow of the team, place people where they belong based on their skills and strengths. Attract new talent by offering a pleasant and well-run organization where staffers are happy. Know who and what you're looking for. Write a specific and detailed job description that leaves no doubt what the position is about. This will weed out unqualified talent.

The job you're looking to hire for should fit in with the organizations policies and procedures. If you're running a youth center, you don't need to hire a senior citizens health administrator -- but you may consider hiring a job skills coordinator who knows how to talk with young people.

People Need Watering Too!

In the bathroom, water goes a long way. It flushes things down in the toilet; it clears away toothpaste and facial products in the sink; and it cleans our bodies in the shower or bath. Yes, water is an essential element in the bathroom. And though it comes and goes, we always want fresh, clean water.

Guess what? In the social profit business, we always want fresh and creative people. Follow me here. I'm not saying change your staff every week but what I am suggesting is that as a leader,

you can give your staff, consultants and volunteers a fresh slate on a regular basis.

My bathroom adventure started when I took a look at what was considered the lowest place in the business model. The relationships I built with my cleaning and maintenance crew became invaluable to how I grew the business forward. It was taking the time with those that were considered the least that gave me the most.

Too many times we create organizational charts that show an infrastructure of who's on top and who's on the bottom. This is the way of most businesses. Unfortunately, we don't examine those charts in terms of people as individuals. We don't realize that it makes one person feel small while another feels empowered.

Consider a different view of your team of people at your social profit organization. With everyone working towards a common goal is there a way you can create

organizational charts that are more empowering?

Following are some alternative organizational charts that have served me well. Note that everyone knows whom he or she report to in terms of supervision, but at the same time everyone is held on an equal footing in responsibility for the organization.

As you put your team together, think of ways that you can empower everyone as part of the team. In doing so you will be watering your garden and the seeds you plant, will take root and grow.

Organizational Charts To Consider

Chapter Three
Running Effective Programs

Bathroom: All plumbing must be working to avoid leaks and problems.

Business: Programs need curricula and evaluative measurements to alleviate problems.

Programs are the heart of why you exist. They should be in sync with your mission to bring your mission to life.

The popular Ted series, that shares information about different ideas, boast a simple two-word mission of Spreading Ideas. Ted eloquently and effortlessly fulfills their mission with programs that allow people to share their ideas across the globe on a staged platform. The programs are conducted in front of live audiences and then posted as videos online. With this

program of hosting Ted Talks, Ted fulfills its' mission of spreading ideas. Even more beautiful, the program is created, implemented and consumed collectively with the organization and its' client base.

How does your mission tie into the work you do? Is everyone on your team in sync with your mission and how it is the catalyst to bring your programs to light? Are your programs clearly outlined so that everyone knows what they are? How do you measure the programs once they are in action? Let's go over some of the program basics through our bathroom analogy.

Who Does Your Program Serve?

Every program is in service to a specific community. It may be based on age, gender, culture or environment. Whatever the population, you have chosen to serve, understand the population demographics. Understand them so much

that you know how and why the program fits with that community.

In the bathroom, we know that each tool is used to serve a distinct purpose. Let's take for example, towels. We know they are used for washing and drying but there are specific towels for specific things. While a washcloth is used to wipe up your face, and overall body parts a hand towel is specifically used to wipe your hands when they are wet. Some use hand towels as a means to actually dry their hair because they are large enough to complete the task, yet small enough not to overwhelm the process. Finally, there's a bath towel, which is created in larger size to be proportionate to your entire body. These are used for drying the complete body.

Just like in the example of towels being specific for bathroom use, so are your programs. Know the demographic

you service and create programs that are specifically catered to them.

What is your program name and purpose?

As you begin to cater your programs to your demographic, consider the naming convention in the same context. As we learned earlier, names are important. Just like a team member needs the appropriate title or name to feel empowered, you want each program to be empowered by name.

Should your demographic be for teenage girls, then relate the name to that segment of the population. A general name like "Basketball / Sports Program" will not fit as well for a demographic specific population. Just adding "girls" to the name distinguishes whom the program is for. Define your programs clearly with the names you use. Next, understand not only what the program name is but also how it relates to those who the program serves.

Let's take the girls basketball program. The name has "Girls and Basketball" included, but what about adding what the program does for the girls who are involved? "Girls Basketball Empowerment," tells me that you're empowering girls through basketball. A title like this lets everyone know the who, what and how that you are serving. If you cannot fit the information describing your program in your title, then think of a good tag line.

A *tag line* is used as a shortened mission statement explaining what the program does in powerful but succinct points. When creating your tagline keep these factors in mind:

- Taglines should work with the program name, positioning and messaging.
- Consistency in messaging is key.

- Use action words in your tagline. Verbs are more powerful to use in taglines than nouns.
- Engage your audience.
- Be Specific and emotive.
- Make it easy to pronounce and spell.
- Make it pleasant to the ear.

Some good examples of social profit names and taglines are:

1. *Sisters4Sisters:* Empowerment of girls and women in mind, body and spirit.
2. *Big Brothers, Big Sisters:* provide children facing adversity with strong and enduring, professionally supported one-to-one relationships that change their lives for the better, forever.
3. *Doctors Without Borders:* Providing Medical Relief Worldwide.

Whatever name(s) you have chosen for your program, should be in alignment with

your actual social profit purpose or mission. Test the name or phrases with constituents before committing and get team involvement. In the end you all have to live with it.

When & How Does Your Program Occur?

Program essentials include the time frame that the activity occurs and how you run the program. If it's that girls' basketball team, when do they meet and how are they organized? Are they a team or do they get coached one on one?

Where do you operate your program?

Do you have a building, are you on-line or do you partner with someone? All of these elements are important to list no your brochure or website so that people understand what you do and how you do it.

Why Does Your Program Exist?

Your program's *"why"* is one of the most important things you will come across. Why do you do the work that you do? Why is the program important? Why is the program relevant for the population you service? Why should anyone fund you?

During a course with the Annenberg Foundation, one of the presenters goes over a process of figuring out each organizations' why. Lawrence Pierce-Durance begins with asking students in the Executive Leadership class to create a case for support of their organization. This is the reason one would support an organization or why the organization exists. The organizations that are participating, usually create cases for support that include the *who, what, when, where and how* of the organization but not the real *"why"*.

At this point, Pierce-Durance asks the leaders to hone in on their case and narrow it down to a 30 second elevator speech.

This makes each leader have to think hard about why the organization is important — more so than what or how they do what they do.

To add "steam" to this nice hot shower of understanding "the why", every time an organization states their "why" -- Pierce-Durance responds with a *"so what?"* This leads the team deeper into their reflection of "why". In the end, a succinct and clear "why" for their existence is developed.

Try this exercise with a partner. Write a case for support, then, see if you can make that case a brief elevator pitch (one to two sentences). Finally, when you have the shortened version, have your partner do the "so what" exercise with you until you get them message tight. You will find this exercise will get you very clear about why you exist.

Pierce-Durance's best example from doing this exercise is from an international organization that provides food to underserved populations to prevent

hunger. After going through the exercise with this organization, the end "why" statement became, "Hunger Hurts." How deeply this message can be felt when presenting to a donor as to why they should support the organization.

Creating the case for support is really something that the entire team can work on. It's part of the work of strategic planning.

Examine your "why?" Make sure it matters.

Summary
People & Programs Together

Bathroom: Exist because people need them.

Business: Exist because the mission is what is needed in the service of the organization & people make it happen.

Bathrooms fulfill an essential life need. Even before indoor plumbing, bathrooms still existed in the form of outhouses. Everyone has always needed a place "to go."

Nowadays, everyone needs a clean, quiet, peaceful place "to go" at some point during the day, and bathrooms fulfill this need.

In the business world, programs exist because of a community need. Whether feeding the hungry, sheltering the

homeless or taking in stray cats — programs are only as good as the people who run them.

Sometimes programs are split into segments or projects. An after school youth center may have Music, Art and Tutoring programs but the major goal is to provide services to youth after school. Whatever the program is, remember to access, measure and evaluate the effectiveness of what you do. Programs are funded for need and success.

Just like in the bathroom, evaluating a best location, size and number of bathrooms, is the best way to plan. To deliver the very best programs and services, use the same philosophy and consider these evaluative steps:

Establish outcome indicators which measure program change. Make your outcome indicators specific, measurable, achievable, realistic and time sensitive (SMART). For example, an outcome of "ESL students become

proficient in English", will show indicators of "The number and percent of students who demonstrate increase in ability to read, write, and speak English by the end of the program."

Track positive and negative results. Resist tracking only the positive, as it does not give your room to improve.

Use donor tools to see results. This includes reviews and evaluations. Ask donors what they use and incorporate.

Evaluation is a mindset that must exist in the whole organization. Everyone should think of outcome data. Once you define goals, give your team the opportunity to determine benchmarks for outcomes.

No matter what your program idea is, ask yourself if it is something the community needs. You need a bathroom, so you build a bathroom. If your community has a large homeless population, open a soup kitchen and homeless shelter. If your community lacks

after school supervision for kids, open a youth program. Find the need and fill it.

Everything in the bathroom has a purpose and a place in order for operations to run smoothly. The toilet paper, plunger, shower curtain, and towel all are placed in strategically to maximize benefit. We don't want any messy clean ups! In business, everyone has his or her place as well.

From the executive director, board chair, board members, and workers, everyone plays an important role. You need to know your role and where you fit in the organization to truly succeed. Using the simple lessons learned in this book will help you manage teams more effectively so that your programs are in order to run your business more efficiently.

Now, get ready to grow your business to the prosperous space you desire.

People & Programs: Social Profit Biz Basics

Everything I Needed In Business I Learned in the Bathroom